Morgan Donovan

How to monetize your x account

A Comprehensive Guide to Monetizing Your X Account

First published by Morgan Donovan 2024

Copyright © 2024 by Morgan Donovan

All rights reserved. No part of this publication may be reproduced, stored or transmitted in any form or by any means, electronic, mechanical, photocopying, recording, scanning, or otherwise without written permission from the publisher. It is illegal to copy this book, post it to a website, or distribute it by any other means without permission.

First edition

This book was professionally typeset on Reedsy
Find out more at reedsy.com

Dedication:

This book is dedicated to all the aspiring creators, entrepreneurs, and influencers who dare to dream big and pursue their passions fearlessly. May you find inspiration, guidance, and empowerment within these pages as you embark on your journey to monetize your X account and turn your dreams into reality. Here's to embracing the power of creativity, perseverance, and determination on the path to success.

Yours sincerely,
Morgan Donovan

"Success is not the key to happiness. Happiness is the key to success. If you love what you are doing, you will be successful."

Albert Schweitzer
Morgan   Donovan

Contents

Foreword 1
Preface 3
Acknowledgement 5
1. Understanding the Potential of X 7
2. Building a Strong Foundation 12
3. Growing Your Audience 17
4. Leveraging Analytics 22
5. Collaborating with Brands 28
6. Sponsored Posts and Ads 35
7. Selling Products and Services 40
8. Leveraging X Spaces and Subscriptions 46
9. Using Affiliate Marketing 52
10. Maintaining and Scaling Your Success 59
11. Appendices 64
12. Conclusion 67
   1.
   2.
   3.
   4.
   5.
   6.

7.
8.
9.
10.
11.
12.
13.
14.

Foreword

Foreword

In today's digital era, the power of social media has transformed the way we connect, communicate, and consume content. Platforms like X have become not just avenues for sharing thoughts and experiences but also lucrative opportunities for monetization. As the digital landscape continues to evolve, navigating the world of social media monetization can seem daunting, but fear not. In "How to Monetize Your X Account" by Morgan Donovan, you'll find a comprehensive guide packed with insights, strategies, and practical advice to help you unlock the full earning potential of your X account.

Morgan Donovan brings a wealth of knowledge and experience to the table, having successfully navigated the complexities of social media monetization and established herself as a trusted authority in the field. Through this book, she shares her expertise, offering valuable insights gleaned from years of hands-on experience and a deep understanding of the ever-changing dynamics of the digital landscape.

From building a strong foundation to leveraging advanced monetization tactics, each chapter is meticulously crafted to provide you with actionable strategies and practical tips that you can implement immediately to accelerate your monetization journey. Whether you're a seasoned influencer looking to diversify your revenue streams or a budding creator eager to monetize your passion, this book is your ultimate companion on the path to success.

I encourage you to dive in, absorb the wisdom contained within these pages, and embark on your journey to monetizing your X account with confidence and clarity. The possibilities are limitless, and with the guidance offered in this book, you'll be well-equipped to seize every opportunity that comes your way.

Here's to your success in monetizing your X account and unlocking a world of possibilities in the digital realm.

[Morgan   Donovan   ]

Preface

Preface

Welcome to "How to Monetize Your X Account" by Morgan Donovan. In this dynamic digital age, where social media platforms have become virtual marketplaces and content creators are the new entrepreneurs, the potential to turn your passion into profit has never been greater. Whether you're a seasoned influencer looking to amplify your earnings or an aspiring creator seeking to monetize your unique voice, this book is your comprehensive guide to unlocking the full earning potential of your X account.

Drawing upon years of experience and expertise in the ever-evolving landscape of social media monetization, I've crafted this book to be your roadmap to success. Through ten meticulously crafted chapters, we'll delve into strategies, techniques, and insider tips to help you navigate the complexities of monetizing your X account with confidence and finesse.

From laying the groundwork with a strong foundation to leveraging advanced tactics like affiliate marketing and subscription models, each chapter is designed to equip you with the knowledge and tools necessary to thrive in the competitive world of social media monetization. Along the way, we'll explore real-life success stories, actionable insights, and practical advice to inspire and empower you on your journey to financial freedom and creative fulfillment.

Whether you're a content creator, influencer, entrepreneur, or anyone with a passion for making a mark in the digital realm, "How to Monetize Your X Account" is your essential companion to turning your dreams into reality. So, buckle up and get ready to embark on a transformative journey that will revolutionize the way you think about monetizing your online presence. The future of your success starts here.

Yours truly,

Morgan   Donovan

Acknowledgement

Acknowledgement:

I would like to express my deepest gratitude to all those who have contributed to the creation of this book, "How to Monetize Your X Account."

First and foremost, I want to thank my readers for their interest and support. Your enthusiasm and encouragement have been a constant source of motivation throughout this journey.

I am immensely grateful to the team at [Publisher Name] for their guidance, expertise, and unwavering commitment to excellence. Your dedication to bringing this project to fruition has been truly inspiring.

I also extend my heartfelt appreciation to [Foreword Author's Name] for graciously providing the foreword to this book. Your words of wisdom and encouragement will undoubtedly inspire countless readers on their monetization journey.

A special thank you to my family and friends for their unwavering support and understanding during the writing process. Your love and encouragement have been my rock throughout this endeavor.

Last but not least, I want to express my gratitude to the countless individuals and organizations whose insights, expertise, and inspiration have shaped the content of this book. Your contributions have been invaluable, and I am deeply grateful for your generosity and support.

Together, we have created a resource that I hope will empower and inspire readers to unlock the full earning potential of their X accounts. Thank you all for being part of this incredible journey.

With heartfelt gratitude,

Morgan   Donovan

1

Understanding the Potential of X

Understanding the Potential of X

Introduction to X

X, formerly known as Twitter, is a powerful social media platform known for its real-time updates, concise posts, and vast user base. With millions of active users worldwide, X provides a unique space where individuals, businesses, and influencers can share ideas, news, and content instantly. The platform's reach and influence have made it an essential tool for communication, marketing, and networking.

User Base: X boasts a diverse and engaged user base, from everyday users to celebrities, politicians, and industry leaders.

Global Reach: X operates in multiple languages and countries, making it a global platform.

Real-Time Interaction: The immediacy of X allows for real-time engagement and trends, making it ideal for timely content and interactions.

Why Monetize on X?

Monetizing your X account can transform your social media presence from a hobby into a lucrative business. Here are some key benefits and potential earnings to consider:

Direct Revenue Streams: Through advertising, sponsored posts, affiliate marketing, and product sales, X offers multiple avenues for direct income.

Brand Partnerships: With a strong following, you can attract brands looking to reach your audience, resulting in paid collaborations and sponsorships.

Content Monetization: Platforms like X Spaces and subscription-based content offer opportunities to monetize your expertise and influence.

Increased Visibility: Monetization efforts often lead to increased engagement and visibility, further expanding your reach and influence.

Potential Earnings: Earnings can vary widely depending on your niche, audience size, and engagement rates. Top influencers can earn thousands of dollars per post, while consistent engagement and strategic partnerships can provide steady income streams.

Success Stories

Learning from successful X account monetizations can provide inspiration and practical insights. Here are a few examples:

1. **Tech Influencer:**

Account: A tech reviewer started by sharing detailed reviews and tech news.

Monetization: Partnered with tech companies for sponsored reviews and used affiliate marketing for tech products.

Outcome: Grew to millions of followers and generated significant income through sponsorships and affiliate sales.

2. Lifestyle Blogger:
Account: A lifestyle blogger focused on fashion, travel, and wellness.

Monetization: Leveraged a strong personal brand to secure partnerships with fashion and travel brands, and created subscription-based content for exclusive tips and behind-the-scenes access.

Outcome: Achieved high engagement rates and a steady stream of income from brand collaborations and subscription fees.

3. Fitness Expert:
Account: A fitness coach shared workout routines, nutrition tips, and motivational content.

Monetization: Offered personalized training programs, partnered with fitness brands for sponsored content, and promoted fitness products through affiliate marketing.

Outcome: Built a loyal community of followers, leading to substantial earnings from multiple revenue streams.

Conclusion

Understanding the potential of X is the first step towards monetizing your account. With its extensive reach, diverse user base, and real-time interaction capabilities, X provides a fertile ground for generating income. By learning from successful accounts and recognizing the various monetization opportunities, you can start your journey towards turning your X presence into a profitable venture.

2

Building a Strong Foundation

Building a Strong Foundation

Defining Your Niche

Identifying your niche is crucial for building a strong foundation on X. A well-defined niche helps you attract a dedicated audience and create content that resonates with them.

Identify Your Interests and Expertise: Start by listing your passions, skills, and areas of expertise. What topics do you enjoy discussing? Where do you have specialized knowledge?

Research Market Demand: Use X's search function, trending topics, and popular hashtags to gauge interest in various niches. Identify gaps in content that you can fill.

Define Your Target Audience: Determine who you want to reach. Consider demographics such as age, gender, location, interests, and behavior patterns.

Select Your Niche: Choose a niche that aligns with your interests, expertise, and market demand. Ensure it's specific enough to attract a dedicated audience but broad enough to allow for varied content.

Optimizing Your Profile

Your X profile is your digital storefront. An optimized profile can attract followers, make a strong first impression, and clearly communicate your brand.

Craft a Compelling Bio: Your bio should succinctly describe who you are, what you do, and what followers can expect from your content. Include relevant keywords to improve searchability. Add a touch of personality to make it unique.

Example: "Tech Enthusiast | Gadget Reviews | Latest Tech News | Helping you stay ahead in the tech world"

Profile Picture: Use a high-quality, recognizable image. If you're a personal brand, a clear headshot works best. For businesses, a logo can be more appropriate.

Header Image: Choose a header image that complements your brand and reinforces your niche. This could be a banner showcasing your products, services, or recent projects.

Pinned Tweet: Pin a tweet that represents your best content, a significant announcement, or a welcome message to new followers. This tweet should encapsulate your brand and encourage engagement.

Content Strategy

A well-thought-out content strategy is essential for maintaining consistency and engagement. It ensures your posts are aligned with your goals and audience interests.

Set Clear Goals: Determine what you want to achieve with your X account. Goals could include increasing followers, driving traffic to a website, or generating sales.

Content Pillars: Identify key themes or topics that you will regularly cover. These should align with your niche and provide value to your audience.

Example: For a fitness account, content pillars could include workout tips, nutrition advice, and motivational stories.

Content Calendar: Plan your posts in advance using a content calendar. This helps maintain consistency and ensures a mix of content types.

Daily Tweets: Post regular updates, tips, or insights.

Weekly Features: Share in-depth posts, videos, or collaborations.

Monthly Themes: Focus on specific topics or campaigns each month.

Engagement Strategy: Engage with your audience by responding to comments, participating in relevant conversations, and retweeting or quoting content from others in your niche. This fosters a sense of community and increases visibility.

Content Formats: Utilize various content formats to keep your audience engaged. This includes text posts, images, videos, polls, and threads. Experiment with different formats to see what resonates most with your audience.

Analyze and Adjust: Regularly review your content performance using X's analytics. Identify what types of content perform best and adjust your strategy accordingly. Stay updated with platform trends and algorithm changes to optimize your reach.

Conclusion

Building a strong foundation on X involves defining your niche, optimizing your profile, and developing a consistent content strategy. By understanding your audience and creating content that resonates with them, you set the stage for successful monetization. A well-optimized profile and strategic content plan not only attract followers but also establish your authority and credibility within your niche.

3

Growing Your Audience

Growing Your Audience

Content Creation

Creating high-quality, engaging content is the cornerstone of growing your audience on X. Here are some tips to help you craft compelling posts:

Know Your Audience: Understand the interests and preferences of your target audience. Tailor your content to address their needs, questions, and interests.

Be Authentic: Authenticity builds trust. Share your unique perspective, experiences, and insights. Avoid overly promotional content; focus on providing value.

Visual Appeal: Use high-quality images, infographics, and videos to make your posts stand out. Visual content is more likely to be shared and engaged with.

Concise Messaging: X's character limit encourages brevity. Craft concise, impactful messages that convey your point clearly and quickly.

Storytelling: Engage your audience with storytelling. Share personal anecdotes, case studies, or success stories that resonate with your followers.

Use Calls to Action (CTAs): Encourage engagement by including clear CTAs in your posts. Ask questions, prompt retweets, or invite followers to visit your website or blog.

Timing and Frequency: Post consistently and at times when your audience is most active. Use analytics to determine optimal posting times.

Utilizing Hashtags

Hashtags are a powerful tool to increase the visibility of your posts and attract new followers. Here's how to use them effectively:

Research Relevant Hashtags: Identify popular hashtags in your niche. Tools like Hashtagify, RiteTag, and X's search function can help you discover trending hashtags.

Mix Popular and Niche Hashtags: Use a combination of widely used hashtags and more specific ones to reach a broader audience while targeting your niche.

Create Branded Hashtags: Develop unique hashtags related to your brand or campaigns. Encourage your followers to use them to increase brand visibility.

Limit Hashtags: Don't overuse hashtags. Stick to 1-3 relevant hashtags per post to avoid looking spammy and maintain readability.

Join Hashtag Trends: Participate in trending hashtags that are relevant to your niche. This can help your content get discovered by a larger audience.

Engagement Strategies

Engagement is key to growing and retaining your audience. Here are some techniques to foster loyalty and interaction:

Respond to Comments and Mentions: Acknowledge and respond to comments and mentions promptly. This shows your followers that you value their input and encourages further interaction.

Host Q&A Sessions: Regularly host Q&A sessions where followers can ask questions about your niche. This positions you as an expert and boosts engagement.

Run Polls and Surveys: Use X's poll feature to gather opinions, feedback, or preferences from your audience. This not only engages followers but also provides valuable insights.

Retweet and Quote Others: Engage with content from other users in your niche by retweeting or quoting their posts. This can help build relationships and increase your visibility.

Collaborate with Influencers: Partner with influencers in your niche for joint content or shout-outs. This exposes you to their audience and can help grow your following.

Share User-Generated Content: Encourage followers to create and share content related to your brand. Feature their posts on your account to build a sense of community and appreciation.

Offer Exclusive Content: Provide your followers with exclusive content, such as behind-the-scenes looks, early access to new products, or special discounts. This rewards loyal followers and incentivizes others to engage more.

Stay Active: Consistency is key. Regularly post and engage with your audience to stay top-of-mind and maintain momentum.

Conclusion

Growing your audience on X requires a combination of high-quality content creation, strategic use of hashtags, and active engagement with your followers. By understanding your audience and providing value through your posts, you can attract and retain a loyal following. Engaging with your audience and leveraging hashtags effectively will help increase your visibility and reach, setting the stage for successful monetization.

4

Leveraging Analytics

Leveraging Analytics

Understanding X Analytics

X provides built-in analytics tools that offer insights into how your content is performing and how your audience is engaging with it. Here's how to navigate these tools:

Accessing X Analytics:
On desktop, click on your profile picture in the upper right corner, then select "Analytics" from the dropdown menu.

On mobile, you can access analytics through the "Profile" section, then click on the "More" button and select "Analytics."

-**Dashboard Overview:**

The dashboard provides a summary of your activity over the past 28 days, including highlights such as top tweets, mentions, and new followers.

The overview page includes metrics like impressions, profile visits, mentions, and follower count.

Individual Tweet Performance:

Click on a specific tweet to see detailed metrics such as impressions, engagements, link clicks, retweets, likes, and replies.

 - This detailed view helps you understand which tweets are performing well and why.

Key Metrics to Track

Understanding and interpreting the key metrics provided by X Analytics is essential for optimizing your content strategy. Here are the most important data points to monitor:

Impressions: The number of times your tweet appeared in someone's timeline or search results. High impressions indicate good visibility.

Engagements: The total number of interactions (likes, retweets, replies, link clicks, etc.) your tweet receives. High engagements suggest that your content resonates with your audience.

Engagement Rate: The percentage of impressions that resulted in engagements. A high engagement rate indicates that your content is compelling to those who see it.

Link Clicks: The number of times links in your tweets are clicked. This metric is crucial if you're driving traffic to a website or landing page.

Retweets: The number of times your tweet is shared. Retweets help increase your reach and expose your content to a broader audience.

Likes: The number of likes your tweet receives. While not as impactful as retweets or replies, likes are a good indicator of content approval.

Replies: The number of replies your tweet gets. Replies foster conversation and can significantly boost engagement.

Follower Growth: The number of new followers gained over a specific period. Monitoring follower growth helps you understand the impact of your content and engagement efforts.

Adjusting Your Strategy

Using the insights gained from analytics, you can refine your content and engagement strategies to improve performance. Here's how to adjust your strategy based on your analytics:

Identify Top-Performing Content: Analyze which tweets have the highest impressions, engagements, and engagement rates. Identify common themes or formats (e.g., videos, images, polls) among your top-performing tweets and create more content in that vein.

Understand Audience Preferences: Look at the types of content that generate the most engagement. Pay attention to the timing, tone, and topics of your most successful tweets to better understand what your audience prefers.

Optimize Posting Times: Use analytics to determine when your audience is most active. Schedule your tweets during these peak times to maximize visibility and engagement.

Test and Iterate: Continuously experiment with different content types, formats, and posting times. Use A/B testing to compare the performance of different approaches and refine your strategy based on what works best.

Engage More Effectively: Monitor which engagement strategies (e.g., Q&A sessions, polls, user-generated content) lead to the highest interaction rates. Focus on the techniques that yield the best results.

Track Progress: Regularly review your analytics to track progress towards your goals. Adjust your strategy as needed to ensure continuous growth and improvement.

Address Underperforming Content: Identify content that doesn't perform well and analyze why. It could be the timing, format, or relevance of the content. Use these insights to avoid similar mistakes in the future.

Conclusion

Leveraging X's analytics tools is crucial for understanding how your content performs and how your audience interacts with it. By tracking key metrics and using the insights gained to adjust your strategy, you can continually refine your approach to maximize engagement and grow your audience. Regularly reviewing and acting on your analytics data will help you create more effective content and foster a stronger connection with your followers, setting a solid foundation for successful monetization.

5

Collaborating with Brands

Collaborating with Brands

Finding Brand Partnerships

Collaborating with brands can significantly boost your income and credibility. Here's how to approach potential partners and what to look for:

Identify Relevant Brands: Look for brands that align with your niche and audience. Their products or services should resonate with your followers and fit naturally with your content.

Research: Use X to identify brands that are already engaging with influencers in your niche. Look at their social media activity, partnerships, and follower interactions.

Industry Connections: Attend industry events, webinars, and conferences to network with brand representatives and other influencers.

Evaluate Brand Fit: Ensure the brand's values, mission, and audience align with yours. Authentic partnerships resonate more with your followers and maintain your credibility.

Audience Demographics: Compare your audience demographics with the brand's target market.

Content Synergy: The brand's products should integrate seamlessly into your content without appearing forced or out of place.

Engage with Brands: Start by engaging with the brand on social media. Comment on their posts, share their content, and mention them in your tweets. This can help you get noticed and build a relationship.

Influencer Platforms: Sign up for influencer marketing platforms like AspireIQ, Influencity, and FameBit. These platforms connect influencers with brands looking for collaborations.

Pitching Your Account

Creating a compelling pitch is crucial for attracting brand partnerships. Here's how to craft a pitch that stands out:

Introduction: Start with a brief introduction about yourself, your niche, and your X account. Highlight your unique value proposition and what makes your content special.

Example: "Hello, I'm [Your Name], a tech enthusiast with a passion for the latest gadgets and innovations. My X account, @[YourHandle], has grown to [Follower Count] followers, who engage with my in-depth reviews and tech news updates."

Audience Insights: Provide insights into your audience demographics, interests, and engagement levels. Use analytics data to back up your claims.

Example: "My audience consists mainly of tech-savvy individuals aged 18-34, with a strong interest in cutting-edge technology and gadgets. My tweets receive an average engagement rate of [X]%, and my followers highly value my product recommendations."

Content Examples: Share examples of successful content that is relevant to the brand you're pitching to. Include links to high-performing tweets, campaigns, or collaborations.

Example: "Here are a few examples of my recent tech reviews and collaborations that have resonated well with my audience: [Link to Tweets]."

Collaboration Proposal: Outline how you envision the partnership working. Be specific about the type of content you will create, the platforms you'll use, and how it will benefit the brand.

Example: "I propose a collaboration where I will create a series of tweets and X Spaces sessions to showcase [Brand's Product]. This will include an unboxing video, a detailed review, and a live Q&A session. This strategy will ensure maximum visibility and engagement."

Benefits to the Brand: Clearly state the benefits the brand will receive from the collaboration. Highlight potential reach, engagement, and the value you bring to the table.

Example: "With my engaged audience and expertise in tech reviews, this collaboration will provide [Brand] with targeted exposure and authentic engagement. My followers trust my recommendations, which can drive interest and sales for your product."

Negotiating Deals

Negotiating terms that benefit both parties is essential for a successful partnership. Here are some tips for effective negotiation:

Know Your Worth: Understand the value you bring to the partnership. Consider your follower count, engagement rates, niche expertise, and past successful collaborations.

Set Clear Objectives: Define what you want to achieve from the partnership. This could include financial compensation, free products, long-term collaboration, or cross-promotion.

Be Transparent: Clearly communicate your expectations regarding deliverables, timelines, and compensation. Transparency helps build trust and ensures both parties are on the same page.

Discuss Deliverables: Agree on the type and number of posts, the platforms to be used, and any additional content (e.g., blog posts, videos). Be specific about deadlines and the approval process.

Compensation: Discuss payment terms upfront. This could be a flat fee, commission-based, or a combination of both. Consider offering packages or tiers to provide flexibility.

Usage Rights: Clarify the usage rights for the content you create. Determine whether the brand can repurpose your content for their marketing channels and for how long.

Contract Agreement: Draft a contract that outlines all agreed terms, including deliverables, compensation, timelines, and usage rights. Ensure both parties sign the contract to formalize the agreement.

Maintain Flexibility: Be open to negotiating terms to reach a mutually beneficial agreement. Flexibility can help build a positive, long-term relationship with the brand.

Conclusion

Collaborating with brands can be a lucrative aspect of monetizing your X account. By finding relevant brand partnerships, crafting compelling pitches, and negotiating beneficial deals, you can create successful and mutually rewarding collaborations. Building strong relationships with brands not only enhances your income but also adds credibility to your influence, further solidifying your presence on X.

6

Sponsored Posts and Ads

Sponsored Posts and Ads

Creating Sponsored Content

Creating authentic and engaging sponsored content is crucial for maintaining your credibility and ensuring successful partnerships. Here's how to do it effectively:

Stay True to Your Voice: Ensure the sponsored content aligns with your usual tone and style. Authenticity is key to maintaining trust with your audience.

Integrate Naturally: Seamlessly incorporate the brand's product or service into your content. Avoid making the post feel like an advertisement; instead, weave it into your narrative or routine.

Example: If you're a fitness influencer, showcase how you use the product in your workout routine rather than just promoting the product.

Focus on Value: Highlight the benefits and features of the product in a way that provides value to your audience. Explain how it solves a problem or enhances their lives.

Use High-Quality Visuals: Invest in high-quality images and videos that capture the product effectively. Visual appeal can significantly impact engagement rates.

Tell a Story: Engage your audience with storytelling. Share a personal experience or a relatable scenario where the product played a crucial role.

Call to Action (CTA): Include a clear and compelling CTA. Encourage your audience to visit the brand's website, use a discount code, or participate in a campaign.

Example: "Check out this amazing product from [Brand] that has transformed my fitness routine. Use my code [CODE] for a special discount!"

Ad Revenue

Understanding and utilizing X's ad revenue sharing programs can be a significant source of income. Here's how to make the most of these opportunities:

X Ads: X allows you to promote your own tweets through its ad platform, increasing visibility and engagement. This can be particularly useful for sponsored content.

Setup: Go to the X Ads platform, create a campaign, and select the tweet you want to promote. Set your target audience, budget, and duration.

Targeting: Use precise targeting options to reach a specific demographic that aligns with your niche and sponsored content.

Monetization Programs: X offers monetization features like Super Follows, Ticketed Spaces, and Tips.

Super Follows: Allows followers to subscribe to your exclusive content for a monthly fee. This can be used to offer premium content, behind-the-scenes looks, or exclusive interactions.

Ticketed Spaces: Charge for access to special audio events. This can be an excellent way to monetize live sessions, interviews, or workshops.

Tips: Enable tips on your profile to receive financial support directly from your followers. This feature allows you to receive monetary contributions for your content.

Disclosure and Transparency

Transparency with your audience is crucial when creating sponsored content. It builds trust and ensures compliance with legal guidelines. Here's how to maintain transparency:

Clear Disclosure: Always disclose when a post is sponsored. Use clear and straightforward language like "#ad" or "#sponsored" at the beginning of your tweet.

Example: "#Sponsored I've been using [Product] from [Brand] and it has made a huge difference in my daily routine! Here's why…"

Honest Reviews: Provide honest and unbiased opinions about the product. Highlight both the pros and cons to maintain authenticity.

Transparency about Partnerships: Be upfront about your partnerships and collaborations. Let your audience know why you chose to work with the brand and how it aligns with your values.

Follow Guidelines: Adhere to the Federal Trade Commission (FTC) guidelines or relevant regulations in your country regarding sponsored content and disclosures.

Example: The FTC requires clear and conspicuous disclosure of material connections between influencers and brands.

Conclusion

Creating sponsored content and leveraging ad revenue opportunities on X can significantly boost your monetization efforts. By crafting authentic and engaging sponsored posts, utilizing X's ad revenue sharing programs, and maintaining transparency with your audience, you can build successful and trust-based partnerships. Transparency and authenticity not only comply with legal requirements but also strengthen your relationship with your followers, enhancing your credibility and long-term success.

7

Selling Products and Services

Selling Products and Services

E-Commerce Integration

Integrating e-commerce into your X account can transform your followers into customers. Here's how to set up a shop or link to your products and services effectively:

Choose a Platform: Select an e-commerce platform that suits your needs, such as Shopify, WooCommerce, or BigCommerce. These platforms offer tools to set up an online store, manage inventory, and process payments.

Create a Shop: Set up your online store with a user-friendly layout. Ensure it is visually appealing and easy to navigate.

Product Pages: Each product should have a detailed description, high-quality images, and pricing information. Include customer reviews if available.

Integrate with X: Link your online store to your X profile to make it easy for followers to find and purchase your products.

Website Link: Include a link to your shop in your X bio.

Pinned Tweet: Pin a tweet that highlights your shop or a specific product, with a direct link to purchase.

Use X Shopping: If available, use X's native shopping features to tag products in your tweets and create a seamless shopping experience.

Promoting Products

Effectively promoting your products on X is essential for driving sales. Here are some strategies to showcase your offerings:

Regular Updates: Consistently post about your products or services. Share new arrivals, special offers, and updates.

Example: "New in stock! Check out our latest [Product Name] now available on our store. Link in bio! #NewArrivals #ShopNow"

High-Quality Visuals: Use high-resolution images and videos to showcase your products. Demonstrate how they can be used or highlight their features.

Example: Create a video showing multiple ways to style a clothing item or a demo of a tech product.

User-Generated Content: Encourage customers to share their own photos and experiences with your products. Retweet and feature these posts to build social proof.

Example: "Love seeing our products in action! Thanks to @User for sharing this amazing photo with [Product]. #CustomerSpotlight"

Special Promotions: Run promotions such as discounts, flash sales, or giveaways to boost interest and urgency.

Example: "Flash Sale! Get 20% off all items for the next 24 hours. Use code FLASH20 at checkout. Link in bio! #FlashSale"

Influencer Collaborations: Partner with influencers in your niche to promote your products. Their endorsement can help you reach a broader audience.

Example: "Excited to partner with @Influencer! Check out their latest review of our [Product]."

Customer Service

Providing excellent customer service is crucial for maintaining customer satisfaction and loyalty. Here's how to manage inquiries and ensure a positive experience:

Prompt Responses: Aim to respond to customer inquiries and comments as quickly as possible. Timely communication shows that you value their business.

Example: "Thanks for reaching out! We'll get back to you within 24 hours. If you have any urgent issues, please DM us."

Clear Communication: Be clear and concise in your communication. Ensure customers understand your responses and any actions they need to take.

Example: "We're sorry to hear about the issue with your order. Please DM us your order number, and we'll resolve it as soon as possible."

Frequently Asked Questions (FAQs): Create an FAQ section on your website or in your X profile to address common questions and issues.

Example: "Check out our FAQ section for quick answers to common questions about shipping, returns, and more: [Link]"

Customer Feedback: Encourage and listen to customer feedback. Use it to improve your products and services.

Example: "We appreciate your feedback! It helps us improve our products and service. Thank you for being a valued customer."

Handling Complaints: Address complaints professionally and empathetically. Offer solutions such as refunds, replacements, or discounts on future purchases.

Example: "We apologize for the inconvenience. We'd like to offer you a replacement or a discount on your next order as a token of our apology."

Conclusion

Selling products and services on X involves effective e-commerce integration, strategic promotion, and excellent customer service. By setting up a user-friendly online store, regularly promoting your offerings with high-quality content, and maintaining responsive and clear customer communication, you can successfully convert your followers into satisfied customers. Providing a positive shopping experience builds trust and loyalty, essential for long-term business success.

8

Leveraging X Spaces and Subscriptions

Leveraging X Spaces and Subscriptions

Hosting X Spaces

X Spaces is a live audio conversation feature that allows you to engage with your audience in real-time. Here's how to make the most of this feature:

Scheduling and Promoting: Schedule your X Spaces sessions in advance and promote them across your X feed and other social media platforms.

Example: "Join me for a live chat on [Topic] this Friday at 5 PM! We'll discuss [specific aspects of the topic]. Set a reminder and bring your questions! #XSpaces"

Choosing Topics: Select topics that resonate with your audience. Consider current trends, frequently asked questions, or areas where you have expertise.

Example: If you're a fitness influencer, topics could include workout tips, nutrition advice, or mental health discussions.

Inviting Guests: Collaborate with other influencers or industry experts to join your Spaces as guests. This can attract their followers to your session and provide diverse perspectives.

Example: "Excited to have @Expert join us for a deep dive into [Topic]. Don't miss out!"

Engagement: Encourage listener participation by opening the floor for questions and comments. This interaction can make the session more dynamic and engaging.

Example: "Feel free to raise your hand if you have any questions or comments. We'd love to hear from you!"

Recording Sessions: Record your X Spaces sessions for those who couldn't attend live. Share the recording link on your X feed and other platforms.

Example: "Missed our live session? Listen to the recording here: [Link]."

Subscription Models

Setting up and promoting subscription-based content can provide a steady revenue stream. Here's how to create and manage subscription models:

Super Follows: Enable Super Follows on your X account to offer exclusive content to paying subscribers.

Setup: Go to your profile settings and apply for the Super Follows feature. Set a monthly subscription fee that provides value to your followers.

Example: "Subscribe for $4.99/month to get exclusive content, behind-the-scenes access, and more!"

Content Tiers: Offer different subscription tiers with varying levels of access and benefits. Each tier should provide increasing value to subscribers.

Example: Basic ($2.99/month) - Early access to new posts; Premium ($4.99/month) - Exclusive content and live Q&A

sessions; VIP ($9.99/month) - One-on-one interactions and personalized advice.

Promotion: Regularly promote your subscription offerings on your X feed and other social media channels.

Example: "Want more exclusive content? Subscribe to my Super Follows and get special insights and tips that you won't find anywhere else!"

Incentives: Offer special incentives for new subscribers, such as discounts, limited-time offers, or exclusive giveaways.

Example: "Subscribe this month and get a 20% discount on your first month! Don't miss out on this limited-time offer."

Exclusive Content

Creating value for subscribers with exclusive offers and content is key to retaining them and attracting new ones. Here are some ideas:

Behind-the-Scenes Content: Share behind-the-scenes looks at your daily life, projects, or how you create your content.

Example: "Exclusive for subscribers: A day in my life video showing how I prepare my content and manage my day."

Early Access: Give subscribers early access to new content, product launches, or special events.

Example: "Super Followers get early access to my latest ebook before it's released to the public!"

Exclusive Tutorials and Tips: Provide in-depth tutorials, tips, or guides that are only available to subscribers.

Example: "Exclusive fitness tutorial just for my subscribers: How to perfect your deadlift technique."

Live Q&A Sessions: Host regular live Q&A sessions where subscribers can ask questions and get personalized advice.

Example: "Join our monthly subscriber-only Q&A session and get personalized answers to your fitness and nutrition questions."

Discounts and Offers: Offer exclusive discounts on your products or services to your subscribers.

Example: "Subscribers get a special 15% discount on all products in my online store!"

Community Engagement: Create a community space for subscribers, such as a private chat group or forum, where they can interact with you and other subscribers.

Example: "Join our exclusive subscriber community on Discord for daily tips, support, and direct interaction with me!"

Conclusion

Leveraging X Spaces and subscription models can significantly enhance your engagement with your audience and provide a steady revenue stream. By hosting engaging live audio conversations, setting up attractive subscription models, and creating exclusive content, you can offer unique value to your followers. These strategies not only increase your income but also deepen the connection with your audience, fostering loyalty and long-term support.

9

Using Affiliate Marketing

Using Affiliate Marketing

Affiliate Programs

Affiliate marketing involves promoting products or services and earning a commission for each sale made through your referral link. Here's how to find and join affiliate programs relevant to your niche:

Research Programs: Identify affiliate programs that align with your niche and audience interests. Look for products or services that you genuinely believe in and that your followers would find valuable.

Popular Affiliate Networks: Platforms like Amazon Associates, ShareASale, CJ Affiliate, and Rakuten Marketing offer a wide range of affiliate programs across various industries.

Direct Programs: Many companies run their own affiliate programs. Check the websites of brands you already use and trust to see if they offer affiliate partnerships.

Apply for Programs: Once you find relevant programs, apply to join them. Be prepared to provide information about your X account, audience demographics, and how you plan to promote their products.

Example: "I'm a fitness influencer with a following of 50,000+ engaged users. I plan to promote your products through dedicated reviews, tutorials, and daily posts on my X account."

Evaluate Terms and Conditions: Carefully read the terms and conditions of each affiliate program. Understand the commission structure, payment methods, cookie duration, and any other relevant details.

Commission Rates: Check how much commission you'll earn per sale. Rates vary widely depending on the industry and product.

Cookie Duration: The length of time a user must make a purchase after clicking your affiliate link for you to receive a commission.

Promoting Affiliate Products

Effective promotion of affiliate products is essential for maximizing your earnings. Here are best practices for promoting affiliate links:

Authentic Recommendations: Only promote products you genuinely believe in and have used yourself. Authenticity is key to maintaining trust with your audience.

Example: "I've been using [Product] for the past month, and it has significantly improved my workouts. Check it out here: [Affiliate Link]"

Create Valuable Content: Integrate affiliate products into your content in a way that provides value to your audience. This can include reviews, tutorials, comparisons, and how-to guides.

Example: "Here's my in-depth review of [Product]. Find out why it's my go-to choice for staying hydrated during workouts: [Affiliate Link]"

Disclosure: Always disclose that your posts contain affiliate links. Transparency builds trust with your audience and ensures compliance with legal guidelines.

Example: "This post contains affiliate links. If you purchase through these links, I may earn a commission at no additional cost to you."

Visuals and Demos: Use high-quality images and videos to showcase the affiliate products. Demonstrate how to use them and highlight their benefits.

Example: "Watch this video to see how I use [Product] in my daily routine: [Affiliate Link]"

Call to Action (CTA): Include clear and compelling CTAs to encourage your audience to click on your affiliate links.

Example: "Ready to try it yourself? Click here to purchase [Product] and take your workouts to the next level: [Affiliate Link]"

Special Promotions: Highlight any discounts, special offers, or limited-time deals to create urgency and drive sales.

Example: "Get 20% off your first purchase of [Product] with code SAVE20! Don't miss out: [Affiliate Link]"

Tracking Performance

Monitoring the performance of your affiliate marketing efforts is crucial for optimizing your strategy and maximizing earnings. Here are tools and strategies for tracking affiliate sales:

Affiliate Dashboards: Most affiliate programs provide a dashboard where you can track clicks, conversions, and commissions. Regularly review this data to understand which products and posts perform best.

Example: "Check your Amazon Associates dashboard to see detailed reports on clicks, ordered items, and earnings."

Link Shorteners and Trackers: Use link shorteners like Bitly or Pretty Links to track the performance of your affiliate links. These tools provide insights into click-through rates and traffic sources.

Example: "Use Bitly to create shortened links for your affiliate URLs and monitor how many clicks each link receives."

Analytics Tools: Utilize analytics tools like Google Analytics to track traffic and conversions on your website or blog if you use these platforms to promote affiliate products.

Example: "Set up Google Analytics goals to track when visitors from your X account make a purchase through your affiliate links."

UTM Parameters: Add UTM parameters to your affiliate links to gain detailed insights into where your clicks are coming from. This is especially useful for tracking the performance of specific campaigns or posts.

Example: "Add UTM parameters like `utm_source=twitter&utm_medium=social&utm_campaign=affiliate_promotion` to your affiliate links."

Review and Adjust: Regularly review your performance data and adjust your strategy based on what works best. Focus on promoting the most successful products and refining your content to better engage your audience.

Conclusion

Affiliate marketing is a powerful way to monetize your X account by promoting products and services that resonate with your audience. By finding and joining relevant affiliate programs, creating authentic and valuable content, and tracking your performance, you can optimize your affiliate marketing efforts and maximize your earnings. Transparency and trust are crucial in maintaining your credibility and building a loyal following, ensuring long-term success in affiliate marketing.

10

Maintaining and Scaling Your Success

Maintaining and Scaling Your Success

Continuous Improvement

Staying updated with platform changes and industry trends is essential for maintaining your success on X. Here's how to continuously improve:

Stay Informed: Regularly check for updates from X and industry news sources to stay informed about platform changes, new features, and best practices.

Adapt and Experiment: Be willing to adapt your content strategy and experiment with new formats, topics, and engagement tactics based on what resonates with your audience.

Learn from Analytics: Use X Analytics and other tracking tools to analyze your performance data and identify areas for improvement. Pay attention to trends and patterns in your audience behavior.

Professional Development: Invest in your skills and knowledge through courses, webinars, and networking opportunities to stay ahead of the curve in your niche.

Community Building

Fostering a loyal community around your brand is key to long-term success. Here's how to build and nurture your community:

Engage with Your Audience: Respond to comments, messages, and mentions from your followers to show that you value their input and engagement.

Create Value: Offer valuable content, insights, and resources that meet the needs and interests of your audience. Solve their problems and address their pain points.

Encourage Interaction: Facilitate conversations and interactions among your followers by asking questions, running polls, and hosting live Q&A sessions.

Reward Loyalty: Recognize and reward loyal followers with exclusive content, giveaways, shoutouts, and special perks.

Be Authentic: Stay true to your brand voice and values, and be genuine in your interactions with your community. Transparency and authenticity build trust and loyalty.

Expanding Your Reach

Scaling your account and exploring new opportunities can help you reach new audiences and grow your success. Here are strategies for expanding your reach:

Collaborate with Others: Partner with other influencers, brands, and organizations in your niche to reach their audiences and gain exposure.

Diversify Your Content: Experiment with different types of content, such as videos, images, infographics, and podcasts, to appeal to a broader audience.

Cross-Promotion: Promote your X account on other social media platforms and vice versa to attract followers from different channels.

SEO Optimization: Optimize your X profile and tweets for search engines by using relevant keywords and hashtags to increase discoverability.

Paid Advertising: Consider investing in paid advertising on X to reach a larger audience and drive targeted traffic to your account and content.

Attend Events: Participate in industry events, conferences, and networking opportunities to connect with influencers, brands, and potential collaborators.

Conclusion

Maintaining and scaling your success on X requires continuous improvement, community building, and expanding your reach. By staying updated with platform changes, fostering a loyal community around your brand, and exploring new opportunities for growth, you can sustain and build upon your achievements. Remember to prioritize authenticity, engagement, and providing value to your audience throughout your journey on X. With dedication, creativity, and strategic planning, you can achieve long-term success and impact on the platform.

11

Appendices

Appendices

Resource List

Affiliate Marketing Platforms: Amazon Associates, ShareASale, CJ Affiliate, Rakuten Marketing.

Influencer Marketing Platforms: AspireIQ, Influencity, FameBit.

E-Commerce Platforms: Shopify, WooCommerce, BigCommerce.

Analytics Tools: X Analytics, Google Analytics, Bitly, Pretty Links.

Paid Advertising Platforms: X Ads.

Glossary

X: Refers to the social media platform being discussed.

Super Follows: A feature on X that allows users to subscribe to exclusive content from their favorite creators for a monthly fee.

X Spaces: A feature on X that enables live audio conversations.

Affiliate Marketing: A marketing strategy where individuals earn a commission for promoting products or services and driving sales through affiliate links.

Engagement Rate: The measure of how actively involved your audience is with your content, often expressed as a percentage.

CTA (Call to Action): A prompt that encourages the audience to take a specific action, such as clicking a link, making a purchase, or subscribing.

UTM Parameters: Parameters added to URLs to track the effectiveness of online marketing campaigns.

Cookie Duration: The length of time a browser cookie remains active after a user clicks an affiliate link, during which the affiliate can earn a commission for any resulting purchases.

SEO (Search Engine Optimization): The process of optimizing your content to rank higher in search engine results pages, increasing visibility and organic traffic.

Cross-Promotion: Promoting one's content, product, or service across multiple platforms or channels to reach a broader audience.

Acknowledgments

Special thanks to [Morgan Donovan team] for their expertise and contributions to this guide.

12

Conclusion

Conclusion

Recap and Final Tips

In this comprehensive guide, we've explored various strategies for monetizing your X account effectively. From building a strong foundation to leveraging affiliate marketing and subscription models, you've learned how to capitalize on your content and engage with your audience in meaningful ways. Here are some final tips to keep in mind:

Know Your Audience: Understanding your audience's preferences, interests, and pain points is crucial for creating valuable content and successful monetization strategies.

Be Authentic: Authenticity builds trust and credibility with your audience. Stay true to your brand voice and values throughout your monetization efforts.

Stay Informed: Stay updated with platform changes, industry trends, and best practices to adapt your strategy and stay ahead of the curve.

Engage Consistently: Regular engagement with your audience fosters a sense of community and loyalty. Respond to comments, messages, and mentions to show your appreciation and build rapport.

Diversify Your Revenue Streams: Explore multiple monetization avenues, such as sponsored content, affiliate marketing, subscription models, and e-commerce, to maximize your income potential and mitigate risks.

Next Steps

Now that you have a solid understanding of how to monetize your X account, it's time to take action. Implement the strategies outlined in this guide, experiment with different approaches, and continuously adapt based on feedback and performance data. Remember that success doesn't happen overnight—consistency, persistence, and continuous improvement are key. Keep creating valuable content, engaging with your audience, and exploring new opportunities for growth. Your journey to monetization success on X begins now!

All Rights Reserved
Morgan Donovan
2024

www.ingramcontent.com/pod-product-compliance
Lightning Source LLC
Chambersburg PA
CBHW050237230526
45470CB00005B/1991